This Amazing World

To Mags N.J. * To D.D. R.R.

Written and compiled by Lois Rock
Illustrations copyright © 2002 Ruth Rivers
Book design by Nicky Jex

Original edition published in English under the title This Amazing World by Lion Publishing, plc, Oxford, England. Copyright © Lion Publishing 2002.

North American edition published by Good Books, 2002.

THIS AMAZING WORLD
Copyright © 2002 by Good Books, Intercourse, PA 17534
International Standard Book Number: 1-56148-363-X
Library of Congress Catalog Card Number: 2002024126

Printed and bound in China.

Library of Congress Cataloging-in-Publication Data
This amazing world / compiled by Lois Rock; illustrated by Ruth Rivers.
    p. cm.
    Summary: A collection of poems expressing thanks and admiration for the world around us.
    ISBN 1-56148-363-X
    1. Nature--Juvenile poetry. 2. Earth--Juvenile poetry. 3. Children's poetry, American. 4. Children's poetry, English. 5. Prayers--Juvenile literature. [1. Nature--Poetry. 2. Earth--Poetry. 3. American poetry--Collections. 4. English poetry--Collections.] I. Rock, Lois, II. Rivers, Ruth, ill.
PS595.N22 T48 2002
811.008'036--dc21   2002024126

Acknowledgments
Every effort has been made to trace and contact copyright owners for material used in this book. We apologize for any inadvertent omissions or errors.

All uncredited poems by Lois Rock, copyright © Lion Publishing.

"i thank You God for most this amazing day" by **E.E. Cummings** is reprinted from *Complete Poems 1904–1962*, by E.E. Cummings, edited by George J. Firmage, by permission of W.W. Norton & Company. Copyright © 1991 by the Trustees for the E.E. Cummings Trust and George James Firmage. "A Prayer for Song Birds" by **Joyce Denha**m, copyright © Joyce Denham, used by permission. "Morning Has Broken" by **Eleanor Farjeon** from *The Children's Bells,* published by OUP, used by permission of David Higham Associates. "Cat" by **Alice Gentry**, copyright © Lion Publishing. "Create a Space" by **Christina Goodings**, copyright © Lion Publishing. "Spell of the Earth" by **Elizabeth Jennings** from *Collected Poems,* published by Carcanet, used by permission of David Higham Associates. "River" and "The Night Watch" by **Mary Joslin**, copyright © Lion Publishing. "Domestic Animals" by Michael Leunig, copyright © **Michael Leunig**, used by permission. "Silver" by Walter de la Mare from *The Complete Poems of Walter de la Mare,* 1969, used by permission of the Literary Trustees of Walter de la Mare and the Society of Authors as their representative. "Weeds" and "The Humbling of Humankind" by **Martin Paul**, copyright © Lion Publishing. "End of Night" and "There Grows a Tree" by **Mark Robinson**, copyright © Lion Publishing. "Harvest Song" and "Moon Mirror" by **Elizabeth Rooney**, used by permission of Patricia Rooney. "I Like the World" by **Steve Turner**, copyright © Steve Turner, used by permission.

This Amazing World

Compiled by Lois Rock

Illustrated by Ruth Rivers

Good Books

Intercourse, PA 17534
800/762-7171 • www.goodbks.com

Rock of Earth

Here on the ancient rock of earth
I sit and watch the sky;
I feel the breeze that moves the trees
While stately clouds float by.
I wonder why our planet home
Spins round and round the sun
And what will last forever
When earth's days all are done.

Spell of the Earth

I am the round of the globe,
The seas are my green robe,
I am where all plants grow
  And the trees know

From me they draw their strength,
From me all stems find length.
I am rich in countless ways,
  All footsteps give me praise.

Elizabeth Jennings

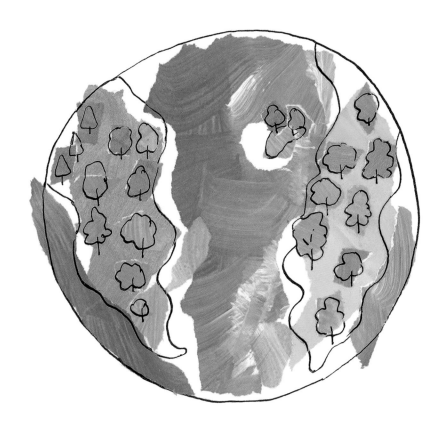

The Great Unseen

I will not hurry through this day!
Lord, I will listen by the way,
To humming bees and singing birds,
To speaking trees and friendly words;
And for the moments in between
Seek glimpses of thy great Unseen.

I will not hurry through this day;
I will take time to think and pray;
I will look up into the sky,
Where fleecy clouds and swallows fly:
And somewhere in the day, may be
I will catch whispers, Lord, from thee!

Ralph Spaulding Cushman

8

This Amazing Day

i thank You God for most this amazing
day: for the leaping greenly spirits of trees
and a blue true dream of sky; and for everything
which is natural which is infinite which is yes

(i who have died am alive again today,
and this is the sun's birthday; this is the birth
day of life and of love and wings: and of the gay
great happening illimitably earth)

how should tasting touching hearing seeing
breathing any – lifted from the no
of all nothing – human merely being
doubt unimaginable You?

(now the ears of my ears awake and
now the eyes of my eyes are opened)

E.E. Cummings

I Like the World

I like the world
The world is good
World of water
World of wood
World of feather
World of bone
World of mountain
World of stone.

World of fiber
World of spark
World of sunshine
World of dark
World of raindrop
World of dew
World of me
and
World of you.

Steve Turner

I Go Forth Today

I go forth today
in the might of heaven,
in the brightness of the sun,
in the whiteness of snow,
in the splendor of fire,
in the speed of lightning,
in the swiftness of wind,
in the firmness of rock.
I go forth today
in the hand of God.

Eighth-century Irish prayer

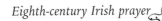

End of Night

At end of night, the sky is dark.
Up from nowhere flies a spark
Of burning gold. It starts a blaze
Among the far horizon's haze;
A fire of red and amber bright
That sets each charcoal cloud alight
And turns the purple and the grey
Into pink and blue of day.
Then rises up the golden O
That shines from heaven to earth below
With power and warmth and light and love
From some great Goodness far above.

Mark Robinson

Morning Has Broken

Morning has broken like the first morning,
Blackbird has spoken like the first bird.
Praise for the singing! Praise for the morning!
Praise for them, springing from the first Word.

Sweet the rain's new fall sunlit from heaven,
Like the first dewfall in the first hour.
Praise for the sweetness of the wet garden,
Sprung in completeness from the first shower.

Mine is the sunlight! Mine is the morning
Born of the one light Eden saw play.
Praise with elation, praise every morning
Spring's re-creation of the First Day!

Eleanor Farjeon

Year

O Year, grow slowly. Exquisite, holy,
　The days go on.
With almonds showing, the pink stars blowing,
　And birds in the dawn.

Grow slowly, year, like a child that is dear,
　Or a lamb that is mild,
By little steps, and by little skips,
　Like a lamb or a child.

Katharine Tynan

Create a Space

Create a space for little things:
Bejeweled bugs with buzzing wings
And pudgy grubs that bravely cling
To slender stems that bend and swing.

Create a calm for quiet things:
For timid birds too shy to sing
And breaths of wind that softly linger
In the blossom trees of spring.

Christina Goodings

15

A Prayer for Song Birds

The God of gods protect you
In wind, and hail, and storm;
In summer, keep you cool;
In winter, keep you warm.

The God of gods supply you
With water and with seed,
With perch and branch and house,
And safety as you feed.

The God of gods be watching,
Lest one of you should fall;
Attending every move;
And hearing every call.

The God of gods uplift you,
And speed you in your flight;
Direct you to a sheltered roost,
And keep you snug at night.

The God of gods inspire you,
And fill your heart with song;
Trill greetings in the morning,
And praises all day long.

Joyce Denham

16

Merry Birds

Merrily, merrily,
All the spring,
Merrily, merrily
Small birds sing.
All through April,
All through May,
Small birds merrily
Carol all day.

Rodney Bennett

There Grows a Tree

There grows a tree
Upon the hill
It bears good fruit
I eat my fill.

There grows a tree
Down by the glade
My love and I
Sit in its shade.

There grows a tree
Within a wood
Its timbers all
Are strong and good.

There grows a tree
Upon the heath
And it will cradle me
In death.

There grows a tree
In paradise
The tree of
Everlasting life.

Mark Robinson

18

Choice of Timber

Choose the willow of the streams,
Choose the hazel of the rocks,
Choose the alder of the marshes,
Choose the birch of the waterfalls.

Choose the ash of the shade,
Choose the yew of resilience,
Choose the elm of the brae,
Choose the oak of the sun.

Carmina Gadelica

Oaks

Great oaks from little acorns grow
And grow and grow
So tall and slow.

From great oaks little acorns grow
They fall below
And grow and grow.

The Forget-Me-Not

When to the flowers so beautiful
The Father gave a name,
Back came a little blue-eyed one
(All timidly it came);
And standing at its Father's feet,
And gazing in His face,
It said in low and trembling tones,
"Dear God, the name Thou gavest me,
Alas! I have forgot."
Then kindly looked the Father down,
And said, "Forget Me Not."

Anonymous

Weeds

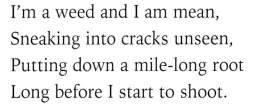

I'm a weed and I am mean,
Sneaking into cracks unseen,
Putting down a mile-long root
Long before I start to shoot.

I rise up from a muddy trench
With a most offensive stench
And terrorize the woodland glades
With leaves as sharp as razor blades.

I raise my gangs of airborne seeds
And train them up for daring deeds,
Telling them the plot we planned
To bind down every grain of sand,

To capture from the sun and rain
The things that make us grow again.
We're the weeds; we really mean
To wrap the whole wide world in green.

Martin Paul

Majesty

I think of the diverse majesty
Of all the creatures on the earth
Some with the power to terrify
And others that only bring mirth
I think of their shapes and their colors
Their secret and curious ways
And my heart seems to yearn for a language
That will sing their Great Maker's praise.

The Humbling of Humankind

When the making of the world was done
and the creatures gathered to see the ones
who, newly formed from dust and clay,
stood all too proudly in the light of day,
they sought among themselves to find
a way to warn that haughty kind.
Soon their choice was made
and Panther slipped out from the shade
and simply stood: black, strong, with fearless eyes.
The people's boasting ceased, and some grew wise.

Martin Paul

Butterfly

Nothing but a butterfly
Can flutter all the day
Where the slender grasses dip
And flowers gently sway
Or tiptoe on the thistledown
Or dance upon the air
Leaving just a ripple
In the golden everywhere.

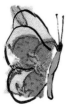

Frog

I'm a frog on a log and I live in a bog
And I jump to the pond, as you know.
But oho and aha! When I'm in the pond
You haven't a clue where I go.

A New Hymn

All things bright and beautiful
All creatures great and small
All weevils, worms and warthogs
The Lord God made them all.

Polar Bear

The polar bear peered from his cave of ice
And began to growl and bellow,
"If God wants me here in a land of snow
Why did he make me so yellow?"

Lion

I am a lion.
I cannot curb
My need to hunt.
Do not disturb.

Penguin

I'm a real penguin.
I'm not fluffy, I'm not sweet.
I'm hungry and ill-tempered
And I've also got cold feet.

Gruffalo the Buffalo

Gruffalo the Buffalo
Was big and brown and hairy.
He went to see a therapist
Because he looked so scary.

He lay down on the prairie couch
And talked for hours and hours.
He said, "The real me is small
And likes arranging flowers."

Domestic Animals

We give thanks for domestic animals. Those creatures who can trust us enough to come close. Those creatures who can trust us enough to be true to themselves.

They approach us from the wild. They approach us from the inner world. They bring beauty and joy, comfort and peace.

For this miracle and for the lesson of this miracle, we give thanks.

Amen.

Michael Leunig

Cat

House cat staring at the starlit sky,
Listening as the breeze goes skittering by,
Do you dream of the monsoon night
Where big cats prowl in the moon's silver light?
Wild and dangerous, solitary, free…
Is that what you are meant to be?

Alice Gentry

Goldfish

Thank you, O Goldfish, for showing to me
The secret life of the silver sea,
For letting me hold, in your fragile bowl,
A tiny drop of the ocean's soul.

What is Pink?

What is pink? A rose is pink
By the fountain's brink.
What is red? A poppy's red
In its barley bed.
What is blue? The sky is blue
Where the clouds float through.
What is white? A swan is white
Sailing in the light.
What is yellow? Pears are yellow,
Rich and ripe and mellow.
What is green? The grass is green,
With small flowers between.
What is violet? Clouds are violet
In the summer twilight.
What is orange? Why, an orange,
Just an orange!

Christina Rossetti

Pied Beauty

Glory be to God for dappled things –
For skies of couple-color as a brinded cow;
For rose-moles all in stipple upon trout that swim;
Fresh firecoal chestnut-falls; finches' wings;
Landscapes plotted and pieced – fold, fallow and plough;
And all trades, their gear and tackle and trim.

All things counter, original, spare, strange;
Whatever is fickle, freckled (who knows how?)
With swift, slow; sweet, sour; adazzle, dim;
He fathers-forth whose beauty is past change:
    Praise him.

Gerard Manley Hopkins

River

Down where the river is quiet and grey
The pull of the current is strong,
Beckoning you on to what might be,
Urging you, "Follow along."

In eddying pools so deep and green
The water now whispers, "Stay!
Safe in the realms of the same as before
And memories of yesterday."

Beyond are the white waves; watch as they curl
And fall in a diamond spray,
"Dare you!" they cry, "Go beyond your dreams,
Do as never before, today!"

Mary Joslin

Caring for the World

Save me a clean stream, flowing
to unpolluted seas;

lend me the bare earth, growing
untamed flowers and trees.

May I share safe skies
when I wake, every day,

with birds and butterflies?
Grant me a space where I can play

with water, rocks, trees, and sand;
lend me forests, rivers, hills, and sea.

Keep me a place in this old land,
somewhere to grow, somewhere to be.

Jane Whittle

Waves

The waves roll in from the glittering green
   of the sparkling summertime sea.
They curl and unfurl on the golden sand
   and run up the beach to me.

The waves roll out to the beautiful blue
   where the ocean touches the sky.
They swish and they slide with the silver tide
   and shyly they say good-bye.

The Silver Road

Last night I saw a Silver Road
Go straight across the Sea;
And quick as I raced along the Shore,
That quick Road followed me.

It followed me all round the Bay,
Where small Waves danced in tune;
And at the end of the Silver Road
There hung a Silver Moon.

A large round Moon on a pale green Sky,
With a Pathway bright and broad;
Some night I shall bring that Silver Moon
Across that Silver Road!

Hamish Hendry

33

The Rainbow

Boats sail on the rivers,
And ships sail on the seas;
But clouds that sail across the sky
Are prettier far than these.
There are bridges on the rivers,
As pretty as you please;
But the bow that bridges heaven,
And overtops the trees,
And builds a road from earth to sky,
Is prettier far than these.

Christina Rossetti

Who Has Seen the Wind?

Who has seen the wind?
Neither I nor you:
But when the leaves hang trembling
The wind is passing through.

Who has seen the wind?
Neither you nor I:
But when the trees bow down their heads
The wind is passing by.

Christina Rossetti

Noise and Stillness

The lightning and thunder
They go and they come;
But the stars and the stillness
Are always at home.

George MacDonald

35

Harvest Song

Sing apples and peaches and pears!
Sing orange and scarlet and yellow!
Sing green turned to glory
To tell us the story
That autumn is merry and mellow!

Sing pheasants and pumpkins and corn!
Sing bonfires and football and raking!
Sing grey misty mornings!
Sing geese calling warnings!
Sing woodpiles and harvests and baking!

Sing holidays, hearth fires and homes!
Sing families loving each other!
Sing closeness, sing dearness,
Sing hearts warmed by nearness!
Sing thanks to our Maker and Brother!

Elizabeth Rooney

The Harvest

The silver rain, the shining sun,
The fields where scarlet poppies run,
And all the ripples of the wheat
Are in the bread that I do eat.

So when I sit for every meal
And say a grace, I always feel
That I am eating rain and sun,
And fields where scarlet poppies run.

Alice C. Henderson

Robin

Robin sang sweetly
In the Autumn days,
"There are fruits for everyone.
Let all give praise!"

Anonymous

November

November is a spinner
Spinning in the mist,
Weaving such a lovely web
Of gold and amethyst.
In among the shadows
She spins till close of day,
Then quietly she folds her hands
And puts her work away.

Margaret Rose

Winter

O thought I!
What a beautiful thing
God has made winter to be
by stripping the trees
and letting us see
their shapes and forms.
What a freedom does it seem
to give to the storms.

Dorothy Wordsworth

The Night Watch

Halt! Who goes there
you shadow-fingered thief,
slipping the gold and velvet of the western sky
under your ragged cloak of grey?

Ha! Do you think you can scare me
with your grim scowl?
Do you even dare step forward
into the fading light?

Oh! Your pardon, great Majesty of Night.
I have for so long kept watch only for the day,
I did not recognize you
in your beggar clothes of evening.

Now I bow before you,
and humbly accept the gifts you kindly bring;
a world of grey and blue, shape and silhouette,
and a silver tracery of glittering constellations.

Mary Joslin

Silver

Slowly, silently, now the moon
Walks the night in her silver shoon;
This way, and that, she peers, and sees
Silver fruit upon silver trees;
One by one the casements catch
Her beams beneath the silvery thatch;
Couched in his kennel, like a log,
With paws of silver sleeps the dog;
From their shadowy cote the white breasts peep
Of doves in a silver-feathered sleep;
A harvest mouse goes scampering by,
With silver claws, and silver eye;
And moveless fish in the water gleam,
By silver reeds in a silver stream.

Walter de la Mare

Moonlight, Summer Moonlight

'Tis moonlight, summer moonlight,
All soft and still and fair;
The silent time of midnight
Shines sweetly everywhere,

But most where trees are sending
Their breezy boughs on high,
Or stooping low are lending
A shelter from the sky.

Emily Brontë

Peace

Peace of the running waves to you,
Deep peace of the flowing air to you,
Deep peace of the quiet earth to you,
Deep peace of the shining stars to you,
Deep peace of the shades of night to you,
Moon and stars always giving light to you,
Deep peace of Christ, the Son of Peace, to you.

Traditional Gaelic blessing

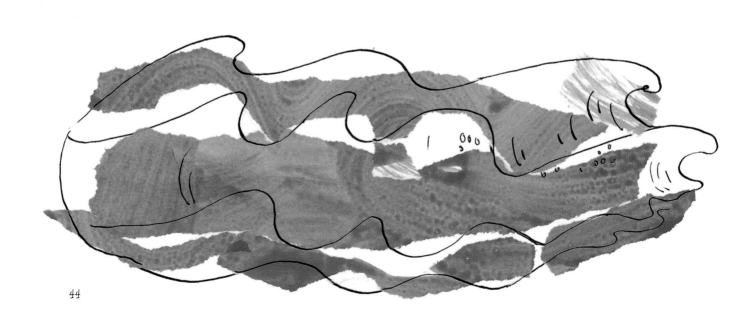

Moon Mirror

Cooled and reflected now,
The hidden sun
Gleams pale as silver
On the shadowed land.
We are not warmed
Yet we are reassured.
Somewhere the sun is shining!
Here, the steadfast stone
Reflects a glory greater than its own
And promises of morning keep
Pouring around us while we sleep.

Elizabeth Rooney

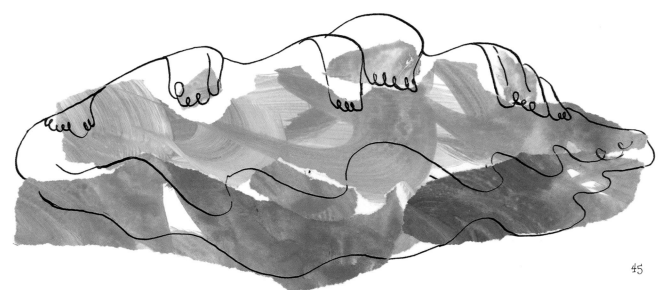

First Lines